DR BOB WOODWARD was born in 1947 in Gloucester, United Kingdom. Having studied at state and Steiner schools, he became a co-worker at the Sheiling School in Thornbury, a centre of the Camphill Community, based on the teachings of Rudolf Steiner (1861-1925). He remained within the Camphill Movement, living with and teaching children with special educational needs, for some forty years, retiring in 2012. He took a special interest in understanding autism in children and young people.

At the age of 46, Bob received an M.Ed degree from Bristol University, followed by an M.Phil at the age of 50 and a Ph.D from the University of the West of England at the age of 64. As well as being a qualified educator, he is a spiritual healer and the author of several books. He is married with five grown-up children and many grandchildren.

D1493805

By the same author:

Spirit Healing (2004)
Spirit Communications (2007)
Spiritual Healing with Children with Special Needs (2007)
Trusting in Spirit – The Challenge (2018)
Knowledge of Spirit Worlds and Life After Death (2020)

Autism – A Holistic Approach
(with Dr Marga Hogenboom) (3rd edition 2013)

JOURNEYING INTO SPIRIT WORLDS

SAFELY AND CONSCIOUSLY

As received through spirit guides

Dr Bob Woodward

CLAIRVIEW

The author encourages readers to make their own choices and decisions in relation to the contents of this book. Any advice, recommendations or teachings given herein should be subject to individual judgement.

Clairview Books Ltd.,
Russet, Sandy Lane,
West Hoathly,
W. Sussex RH19 4QQ

www.clairviewbooks.com

Published by Clairview Books 2022

A CIP catalogue record for this book is available from the British Library

ISBN 978 1 912992 36 2

Cover by Morgan Creative
Typeset by Symbiosys Technologies, Visakhapatnam, India
Printed and bound by 4Edge Ltd, Essex

CONTENTS

DEDICATION

To my very good friend Neil Castleton who passed into spirit on 21 August 2019 when not quite 53 years old. Neil and I had many conversations concerning spiritual perceptions and experiences, based on his own personal knowledge. He was someone who knew of spirit worlds through his conscious, out-of-body journeys into those differentiated dimensions of reality. He also conducted fascinating original research into the dynamics and structure of the human energy field, or aura. I feel extremely grateful to have known Neil in this present lifetime, though I also believe we have shared earlier incarnations together. He was, and is, a true friend. Thank you!

ACKNOWLEDGEMENTS

Many thanks to Hazel Townsley who typed my original handwritten manuscript into a clear and readable form. She has done such tasks for me over many years, and without her dedicated help it is difficult to imagine how I could possibly have managed to complete all my various projects. Thank you, Hazel! Also, thanks to my friend Pete Newberry ('Peter John') for his enthusiastic support for my work with my spirit guides.

Many thanks finally to Sevak Gulbekian and the team at Clairview for taking on to publish this new book. Sevak's phone call, which came just a few days after him receiving the manuscript, caught me by surprise to learn that he was keen to publish it! His feeling that this should be a good addition to my previous book, *Knowledge of Spirit Worlds and Life After Death*, led me to readily agree to his offer.

I do think that things have a way of coming about, sometimes quickly, when the time is right for them.

Dr Bob Woodward
October 2021

FOREWORD

Bob uses an easy-to-follow dialogue with his spirit guides. The way he works with them is so perfectly simple and easily understood.

These liaisons Bob has with his spirit guides are, however, profound and uplifting. The reassurance they bring us about the 'Afterlife' is unique and compelling. I love the reference to 'imagination', and the influence of imagination as a tool for all us earthbound souls to use when communicating with spirit guides.

We should trust our imagination more, and Bob and his spirit guides infer this in this splendid work.

Peter John
Psychic Artist

1.
INTRODUCTION

My reason for writing this book is quite simple. I want to ask my spirit guides (see Appendix 1) to tell us of ways in which we can safely and consciously enter into spirit worlds. In other words, how we may already, whilst still living in our physical bodies on Earth, cross over the threshold which leads into realms of spirit. As a lifelong pupil of the works of Rudolf Steiner, the Austrian spiritual scientist, I am familiar with the esoteric pathways which he described in order to gain personal knowledge of higher worlds. For example, in his seminal book *How to Know Higher Worlds** he writes that,

> In ancient, prehistoric times, the temples of the spirit were outwardly visible, but today, when our life has become so unspiritual, they no longer exist where we can see them with our physical eyes. Yet spiritually they are still present everywhere, and whoever seeks can find them.

(Steiner, 1994, p.16)[†]

In addition to this early fundamental 'handbook', Steiner also gave, towards the end of his life, other esoteric contents designed to enable the aspirant to gain deep spiritual experiences.

However, these anthroposophical pathways probably are not for everyone, in the sense that many people may

---

* Also published under the title *Knowledge of the Higher Worlds*.
[†] See Further Reading on p. 88 for all references.

1

find them too inaccessible and arduous. Whilst Steiner asserted, one hundred or so years ago, that these paths were indeed appropriate for people of our modern times, it seems to me that there must also be other, equally valid, meditative ways to gain entrance to these higher worlds; ways that are perhaps more accessible for ordinary people, who are serious seekers after truth, and who also wish to gain a greater sense for the meaning and purpose of their own lives. It is therefore out of this specific motivation, and in a spirit of service, that I will ask the guides to give us the benefit of their own teachings and advice.

Exactly where this advice will lead us, and just how it will lead us, I cannot yet say. However, I am looking forward to see what will come from the guides when, working together, we begin to explore the way, or ways, to enter spirit worlds. This particular, experiential theme, is rather different from the work which I have done previously with my guides, as expressed in the books so far published, namely,

- *Spirit Communications* (2007)
- *Trusting in Spirit – The Challenge* (2018), and
- *Knowledge of Spirit Worlds and Life After Death* (2020)

However, I believe it is the next obvious step to take: not just simply bringing through the teachings from the guides to help us steer a course through our earthly lives, or to learn from them of spirit worlds *per se*, but now to actually chart a way for us to also gain our own direct knowledge of the worlds in which they, as guides, live. These are, I believe, the same worlds which we will enter into after our earthly deaths and, indeed, the very same worlds from which we have also descended into our earthly births.

2

We now live in times when many people feel there is an urgent need to reconnect consciously with these spiritual realms, because only then will we actually discover who we are in our real selves. That is to say, as veritable spirit beings in our own divine right. Ultimately, entering into spirit worlds will therefore bring us true knowledge of ourselves and, through this revelation, we will be better able to work as enlightened spirits to further the good of the whole world. We will be able to see everything in a new and more compassionate light.

Real knowledge overcomes ignorance and fear and it is these two hindrances which impede all genuine human progress. On the other hand, true insight leads to a wholesome love of ourselves, of others, and of our endangered planet. It leads also to true freedom, not just political or social, but to an inner freedom of the soul and spirit. I believe that freedom and love are the twin goals of our earthly evolution, which can inspire us to courageously walk the paths to the spirit.

This volume might perhaps be referred to as a 'channelled' book. But what is meant by this, other than saying that it is guided by spirit? If those in spirit were not willing to cooperate in bringing this book about then the project would not be possible. Why? Because it is precisely their guidance, their teaching, their advice, which we are seeking here in order to discover pathways to enter into spirit worlds. In this sense, I believe, this book has a certain uniqueness – not least because, as the scribe, I do not yet know what will actually be given in the chapters that follow. It will, therefore, be a 'work in progress', step-by-step.

This is of course not the first so-called 'channelled' book. Probably there are very many. However, there are, I think, important distinctions to be made in how this particular label, or characterization, is made. For me, the most important issue concerns the specific methodology employed in bringing through the inspired contents. Therefore, let me first make as transparent as I can, what is involved in my communicating with my spirit guides and in translating into script the thought contents so given.

Essentially, I describe this form of communication by using the term 'mental telepathy'. By this I mean a direct transfer of thoughts from each of the guides into my mind. It is a conscious process of thought transference, in which I remain in control of my normal thinking capacities and self-consciousness. No trance states are involved, with no lowering of either my mental capabilities or my self-awareness. This is, I feel, very important, because, as a lifelong student of Rudolf Steiner's anthroposophy, I set great store on 'thinking' as a spiritual activity. That is to say, thinking *per se* as a creative ability, which should not be confused with having purely intellectual, logical or abstract thoughts.

In order to receive the contents coming from the guides I have had to learn, over the past fifteen years, to clearly distinguish my own thoughts from those which are given to me. In such mental telepathy, I am suspending my own thinking activity when receiving the thoughts from the guides. I am then allowing the guides to think in me. In practise, the distinction between the two sources, myself or a guide, becomes immediately evident when I am engaged in putting words on paper. If I am myself composing a chapter then I have to engage my own thinking and, mostly, this is hard work! In contrast, when I allow a guide to give me his or her thoughts, the flow of words is effortless and fluent. However, this is not to be construed

4

as so-called 'automatic writing' where a medium, often in some degree of trance, allows his or her hand to simply be moved by spirit control. In such cases, the medium may have absolutely no idea what has been written, until this is subsequently reviewed. In other words, the contents are received largely, or completely, unconsciously. Nothing could be further removed from my own work with the guides, because a fully conscious cooperation in thought transference takes place between us.

I also do not engage in any special breathing techniques or meditations, nor do I sit in any particular posture when communicating with friends in spirit. In fact, I simply sit at my desk as I would to write a letter. However, I do put myself into an open and receptive state of mind, with an inner listening gesture, and then refrain from thinking my own thoughts. Very importantly, I exercise trust towards the guides, as they do towards me. Such trust is not in any way a blind faith. Neither is it an unthinking acceptance of what is received and committed to paper. Yes, it is true to say that I do not know beforehand what the guides will actually say. However, this is no different to when we are having a conversation with another, physical, person. We also do not know beforehand what he or she will say to us, although we might, perhaps, reckon to have a good idea of this. 'Yes, I thought you might say that.' This intuitive ability will probably depend on how well we can 'tune-in' with our conversation partner. Similarly, this will often be my experience when speaking with one or the other of my spirit guides. On the other hand, something may be communicated which I did not at all anticipate or expect. It has been my usual practice to actively question and query, for the sake of clarification and transparency, whatever the guides have said. If, for example, a teaching has first been given, then this is followed by a conversation in the form of a question-and-answer session. This practice is, I think, perhaps not typical of many 'channelled' books, when alleged spirit teachings have been received.

My assumption in writing this introduction is that the guides I have already worked with will also be the ones who will cooperate in creating this one. I will see if this assumption proves correct by 'sensing' who steps forward to contribute. Perhaps one or the other new guide will appear. I am open to that possibility. So at this stage I do not know anything about the form and construction of this new book. I will allow the chapter headings to emerge step-by-step. I also do not know whether the guides would simply prefer to give their own teachings about the pathway into spirit worlds, or whether they prefer conversations to be the format. Perhaps, as in my previous books, both forms will be most appropriate? This question is as good a place to start as any, so, without further ado I will now ask my main guide, Joshua, what he and the other guides want: teachings or conversations, or both?

Bob: Joshua, you already know the question, so can you give me an answer on behalf of yourself and the other guides, please?

Joshua: Shalom, my friend. Yes, I can. We would prefer to first give teachings and then for a conversation to ensue on the basis of what has first been given. Is this alright with you?

Bob: Yes, Joshua, I am happy to work like this. Will you, as guides, also give me a title for each chapter as we proceed with the book?

6

Joshua: Shalom, my friend. Yes, we will. Do not rack your brains about this, we will give a clear title for each chapter.

Bob: Thank you, Joshua. Will it be the same eight guides that have worked with me on the previous two books, or will there be some changes?

Joshua: Let us see. Because we are going to take up a new theme, namely: 'The path, or way, to gain safe and conscious entry into the spirit worlds', we will see who is best suited to do this task with you. We suggest that you be open to sense who wants to come through, by receiving the name of that guide. We are looking forward to this enterprise. It is a challenge for us, as also for you and your readers, if you and they actually take up our suggestions.

Bob: Right, Joshua, I think I will bring this short introduction to a close and be ready to begin the chapter concerning this pathway to the spirit in our next session.

Joshua: Good, we look forward to this.

*

So, there we have it. We will see how the guides can help us to find a way in which we can raise our consciousness to enter safely into those worlds which, I believe, are linked with our physical plane, and in which we can discover who we really are. However, let us keep clearly in mind that this book is intended for anyone, including followers of any particular faith, church, religion, esoteric school, or arcane organization. It is for anyone and everyone who, in all sincerity, wishes to learn how to step beyond our everyday reality, into different and more spiritual dimensions.

This book specifically aims to help meet such seekers' practical need for guidance and clear instruction in this quest. I look forward to see how this will unfold. It is important to say that I have not edited any communications from the guides. They are reproduced verbatim, just as they were received by me. So, let us now begin this adventure and exploration together.

2.
PREPARING TO ENTER
THE PATHWAY

Prologue

Bob: So, Joshua, I am sat down this morning and ready to begin this chapter and see where it will lead us on our journey towards conscious entry into spirit worlds. Are you and the other guides ready to work with me?

Joshua: Shalom, my friend. Yes we are. As we agreed yesterday, one of the guides will step forward and first give a 'teaching' to which you can then open up a question-and-answer session. In that conversation other guides may wish to contribute, as well as the particular guide whose teaching has come first.

Bob: Right, Joshua, let's see who wants to get the ball rolling, so to speak.

Red Cloud: Bob, I will give the teaching for this chapter of the book.

Teaching

Red Cloud: Now, in the first place let me say that before embarking on any journey – or adventure, we could say – due preparations are needed. It would be foolish to set out on a journey without giving careful consideration to how best to go about this, and how best to equip oneself to be able to succeed in the task at hand. So, this is the first thing for us to turn to and to ask the question, 'What sort of preparation is required by someone who wishes to gain safe and conscious entry into spirit worlds?'

The preparations required are those of heart and mind. By this I mean that anyone who sincerely wishes to be able to cross over the border, the boundary, the threshold, between the worlds, must approach this task with clarity of heart and mind. It is no use having vague aspirations or having unclear notions of what is proposed and intended. It is after all a very significant step to make, because in ordinary life on Earth, on the physical plane of existence, this step is not made consciously. True, every night and indeed every time you drop off to sleep, you loosen yourselves from your physical, material bodies, and cross over the threshold. However, this is not a conscious crossing. It is an automatic one that happens simply because, through fatigue say, you are ready for a break; a break from the demands and stimulation of everyday life. Therefore you go to sleep, and in sleep you drift here or there but, usually, without any clear awareness of exactly where you now are. The task we have in this book is to help you to gain clarity, to gain conscious awareness of the state you are in when you cross over – when you make the journey into spirit worlds.

So, coming back again to the matter of due preparations, let me say the following. It is necessary in the first place to begin to train yourself in the matter of gaining inner quiet. This is easy to say but rather difficult to do! It is difficult because for most people their minds are a hive of activity, like bees buzzing around all over the place. However, to keep that analogy for a moment, bees actually know what they are up to. They follow a plan and each bee in the hive knows the task to be performed. Therefore, what can appear to the casual observer as chaos is, in reality, a planned enterprise by the whole colony of bees. Now, in a similar way we could say: it is necessary for the one who wishes to enter consciously into spirit worlds to bring their mind into order, into a harmonious way of working. This is the opposite of chaos.

Now when I say 'mind' this should not be seen in too narrow a sense. I mean rather the whole person in his or her inner soul nature. It is a matter of bringing the soul into proper shape and order. How can this be done?

Well, now we have to turn to specific exercises, shall we say, specific practices that can facilitate this process. I mean such exercises as those with which you are already familiar. Namely control of thoughts, feelings and actions. By control I do not mean some sort of external mechanism but I refer, of course, to the sort of control which you can practise inwardly through self-observation and self-reflection. It is as though you acquire the habit of holding a mirror up to yourself; of looking at yourself from outside, so to speak, in order to gain a clearer picture of what is really going on inside you. From the points-of-view of the Native American traditions that I was once embedded in, in my earlier lifetime with the Sioux, I would have to describe what I am proposing as a sort of 'purification process' – a sorting out of the wheat from the chaff. A distilling of the heavier substances from the finer, lighter ones. This is what I mean by a purification process.

Now, I do not expect you, my friend, or anyone else for that matter, to suddenly imagine that they have to completely transform or purify themselves in order to set out upon the journey – a journey of a lifetime, you might say. No, it is a gradual process, a daily working, a discipline, that is required, like the slow dripping of a tap that gradually smooths the roughness of the stone. This requires, above all else, patience and perseverance. It is not something that can happen overnight. It is a determination to prepare oneself in heart and mind to gain clarity and control of one's thoughts, feelings or, better said, one's emotions and actions. The whole point of this is to gain the necessary balance and self-control when you no longer have the benefit of your physical body to hold everything together for you. On Earth it is your body which is the anchor. It keeps you grounded, and also provides the vessel or container for your soul-functions. When you leave your body behind, in order to enter consciously into spirit worlds, then you need to have gained sufficient mastery of your soul-forces in order to hold yourself together as a free being. This is the great challenge. If you really do want to make this journey into other dimensions of existence safely and surely, then preparation and discipline are absolutely necessary. It is no use leaving the safety and security of the earthly realm without having equipped yourselves properly for the way ahead. No explorers in their right minds would wish to set out recklessly on a perilous journey without having done all that was needed beforehand. So, my friend, this is the first thing to point out to you and to the readers of this new book. Prepare yourselves carefully before setting out on your quest. This is not delaying what you want to achieve. It is about ensuring that you can be – will be – successful in the enterprise before you. All who have followed before you into spirit worlds know the wisdom of preparation – they know that this is the very first step on your journey.

All blessings, Red Cloud

Questions

Bob: So, Joshua, I turn to you first this morning as my main guide, to see who wishes to step forward to answer my questions concerning the teachings which Red Cloud gave yesterday. Who, Joshua, wants to step forward now?

Joshua: Shalom, my friend. Raja Lampa is very keen to step forward first and begin to answer whatever questions you may have.

Bob: Right. So, my first question is: 'How long is this preparation that Red Cloud talked about going to take – days, weeks, months, years'?

Raja: It will take as long as it needs in order to prepare the person to gain safe entry to spirit worlds.

Bob: Alright, but this doesn't give me or the readers any clear timeline, does it?

Raja: The timeline you want will vary from person to person. This is entirely individual. It is a question of achieving sufficient inner control, sufficient inner mastery of the functions of the soul, before actually making the crossing. Think of it as getting everything shipshape, so to speak, before setting out on a voyage of discovery. If the ship and its contents have not been put

13

into good order before setting sail, then you may well break down and grind to a halt before getting very far! Now, this is to be avoided at all costs. The whole point of the voyage, of the journey, is to be ready to enter into new dimensions of experience, or reality, and you simply cannot do this if your soul-life is a mess! It first has to be tidied up and made fit for purpose.

Bob: Very well, Raja, but can you now give some clear practical directions, exercises, for doing this; for getting ourselves sorted out for this endeavour?

Raja: Yes, I can. You must of course start with your thinking – with your thoughts. If your thoughts are all the time scattered here and there and everywhere, then you will have no means of focussing yourselves on the other side of the threshold, that is, in spirit worlds. Your thinking needs to acquire power and strength. Ordinary thinking is far too sloppy, too lazy, too inefficient, to provide the power which you will need when freed from your physical body. Remember, my friend, that the inner training which you undertake has the purpose to bring everything into harmony and balance, before you embark on your journey beyond the threshold that separates the physical from the spirit worlds. Therefore, much care and attention needs to be given to your preparation beforehand.

Bob: Alright, Raja, I can accept, and see, what you are saying. However, we need clear definite exercises, trainings, to achieve what you are saying. Can you give us these?

Raja: Well, I will try to. As I have said, the first thing to gain is some control over your thinking. You need to practice focussed attention. By this I mean really centring your attention, your concentration, we could say, upon whatever subject you choose to focus on. Your ability to do this should grow from strength to strength, if you practise it! This is the first thing. Then you also need to gain control and discipline over your feelings, drives, desires, passions, etc. – all that is contained in your life of emotions. Above all, you must desist from simply reacting to situations that formerly would have caused irritation, frustration, anger, annoyance, jealously, hatred, etc., etc. You understand what I mean? A deep tranquillity of soul must replace all that formerly could drive you to distraction. A deep peace must enter your soul-life, in which you can come to rest; a rest such that it provides a new and sure ground under your feet. It should be a solid foundation compared to the choppy waters of your emotions. Then, the other thing which you need to learn is to do what you say you will. That is to apply yourself, through your willpower, to the tasks which you give yourself to do. Not to say, 'Oh, I forgot to do that, I'll do it tomorrow instead'. No, now you need to train yourself to take yourself in hand, so to speak, and really do the task or tasks which you have set yourself. In this way, you will become strong and be able to see through what you set before yourself to do.

Bob: Well, Raja, I am of course familiar with the things you are talking about through my study of Rudolf Steiner's writings about the path of inner development.

Raja: Quite so. We realize that this is familiar territory for you, but it may be quite new to those who know nothing of Steiner's writings.

Bob: Yes, indeed it may. Raja, is there anyone else who wants to contribute to this conversation?

Raja: Yes, there is. Philip, your angel, wishes to step forward now.

Bob: Right, I will have a short break and then be open for what Philip wishes to share.

Bob: So, Philip, can you help elucidate what Raja was saying about gaining control over our inner life of soul?

Philip: Yes, Bob, I can. It is necessary that, as human beings, you learn to take yourselves in hand, in the sense that your forces, your soul-powers, we can say, become tools for you. Tools in the sense that you can make use of them freely, instead of being enslaved by them. People are far more limited by their own inner life than they will readily admit. However, those of us who live permanently in spirit can see what chaos ensues from souls that are undisciplined and run riot. We do not mean to criticize with this. We respect the free will and choices of human beings, but it is a question of learning to use the powers which you have for your own true benefit, as well as for the universe as a whole. That is why it is really so essential that in order to cross over the threshold between the sense world, the world of physical senses, into the spirit world, that you bring your inner powers into order and harmony. The more harmonious they become, the better able you will be to orientate yourselves correctly, to integrate yourselves properly, into the new dimensions which you enter into. In short, if you bring chaotic forces across the threshold, then you will be in a far worse state of being than you are in ordinary, physical life. This is why your inner training is so essential before you leave the safe ground, comparatively speaking, of your ordinary life on Earth.

Bob: Very well, Philip, the point you make is understood. Have you any further advice in terms of preparations for this journey?

Philip: My friend and brother, it is our earnest wish as spirit beings to be of service to you who live in earthly incarnation. So, in addition to the work which you do to train yourselves in your thoughts, feelings and actions, we would say, develop feelings of reverence and humility towards the beings who seek to help and guide you. Guidance is being given, even if you are unaware of it. You are watched over and helped in many unseen ways. The more you can become conscious of these positive supports and helpful influences, the better this enables you all to make progress in the right direction. Ask for the help you need if you are really sincere in your quest, and then this help will be forthcoming. Many beings are interested when human beings are sincere in their quest to enter spirit worlds, consciously and cooperatively.

Bob: Thank you, Philip. I now wonder if we can pass on to the next chapter, though I don't yet know what its title is. Joshua, can you give this title, heading or theme?

Joshua: Shalom, my friend. Yes I can. Let's call it, 'Stepping over the Threshold'.

Bob: Joshua, is this not going too far already?

Joshua: No, it isn't, as you will see when the teaching is first given.

3.
STEPPING OVER THE THRESHOLD

Prologue

Bob: Joshua, I am once again ready to work with you and the other guides on this theme of learning how to cross the threshold consciously and safely. Are you and the others ready and willing to cooperate with me on this?

Joshua: Shalom, my friend. Yes we are and it is indeed Markos who would like to be the one to first give the teaching on this theme for today.

Bob: Right. So, Markos, the title of this chapter is 'Stepping over the Threshold'. Can you give your teaching on this please?

Markos: Yes, I can do so.

Teaching

Markos: In the first place, let me say that stepping over the threshold between the physical – or material – and the spirit world is something which each of you do at least once a day, and sometimes more often. You do this every time you fall asleep. So you see, it is actually something with which you are all very familiar. The problem is that when you fall asleep you also lose your self-awareness and your normal consciousness. You plunge then into darkness as far as your light of thinking is concerned. You literally are like a blind man who has no idea of what is around him in the daylight world. You are effectively blinkered and unable to know, through your own perception, the new dimensions into which you have entered through going to sleep, i.e. through leaving your physical bodies. So, the challenge my friends is how are you going to be able – to be enabled – to gain clear awareness of where you are once you have exited your physical bodies. This is the great challenge with which you are faced because, you see, it is only the fact that you lack the inner strength, the inner discipline, to wake yourselves up on the other side of the threshold which prevents you from knowing where you are. So the question is: 'How can you learn to do this?' To wake up to clear consciousness when you are out of your bodies, i.e. your physical, material bodies. This is the theme we will examine today.

So, the task is to gain the necessary strength of soul, strength of mind, to remain awake in your awareness when you no longer have the physical body, and the brain in particular, to act as a mirror for your perceptions. This is what is happening in your normal, daily physical existence. Your brain acts exactly like a mirror, which then reflects back to you your perceived surroundings. It also reflects back to you an image of yourselves, so that you have self-consciousness or self-awareness. When you leave your physical body behind, and this of course includes your physical, material brain, then you no longer have the benefit of this reflecting organ. You have relinquished the mirror which, normally, you hold up to yourselves in order to gain self-perception and, together with it, world-perception. So, my friends, the question is: 'What can you do to replace this mirror when you are no longer in your bodies?' The answer to this question rests entirely on the inner work you can do to build a new mirror for yourselves. This new mirror has to be fashioned by yourselves; it is not given to you by nature, so to speak, but needs to be formed through your own construction, your own building capacity. The tools you need to do this task are what you know in terms of meditation and inner, mental, activity. However, by mental activity I am not referring to your normal intellectual activity, which is entirely bound to the physical brain-mirror. No, I mean a mental, or spiritual, activity which takes its stand by means of the effort which you put in to develop your own organ of reflection. This is a spiritual and not a material organ. It is the organ which you need to develop for yourselves, if you are going to perceive the spirit world around you. So, my friends, this is the task which stands before you, if you sincerely want to now step over the threshold between the material and the spiritual worlds, in full consciousness and full awareness. This is the challenge which everyone who has ever wanted to wake up to the spirit realizes – the challenge that human beings have had to face. This is what I wanted to bring to you today, as the teachings which belong to this particular chapter of our book. In other chapters we will elaborate exactly how to do the necessary work, how to do the necessary inner training, which will allow this new organ of perception to develop within your heart and mind. In effect, you will need to create spiritual eyes and ears if you are to learn to see and hear in the worlds of spirit beings.

All blessings, Markos

Questions

Bob: Joshua, I turn to you again as my main guide to ask if Markos, or perhaps other guides, are now prepared to answer my questions about this teaching?

Joshua: Shalom, my friend. We are all ready to help you with the questions you have. So simply ask and then see which of your guides will step forward first.

Bob: Right. Well, my first question is this. If indeed it is true that we need to develop a new organ (or perhaps organs) to be aware of the spirit worlds when we exit our bodies, e.g. during sleep, how do we practically go about acquiring these organs?

Joshua: Shalom, my friend. Let me step in here to answer your question. So, in the first place we need to keep in mind what we said before in the previous chapter, namely the necessity of learning, gradually, to gain greater control of your three soul-functions or capacities. Namely, your thinking, feeling and will. In ordinary life on Earth these capacities are not well developed, in the sense that they remain rather undisciplined. By this I mean that they are left to run their course without much inner direction. The direction they do have is largely provided by the various outer necessities of life. Yes, you have to get out of bed in order to get yourself ready to go to work. This is the typical situation. Therefore, you spring into action, or more slowly, simply because the outer world demands this of you. And so it is with most things which you meet during your daily life. Life itself determines how you think, act and feel. You yourself, as a spirit being – which is what you actually are – are acting in daily life like a puppet on a string. Your actions follow from all that life expects and demands of you. Yes, you do of course also have your times of leisure and recreation, but even in these moments your actions are very much determined, or at least influenced, by the outer necessities of life. Now, my friends, for developing the organs which Markos has referred to, quite different demands need to be made upon you. However, these demands are self-inflicted, so to speak – only you put these demands upon yourself. Therefore, to go along this path of self-discipline, of self-training, is something you are free to choose or not to choose. The choice is truly your own.

Bob: Right, Joshua, I understand what you are driving at, but can you be more precise about what we actually need to do to gain the strength to wake up, so to speak, when out of our bodies?

Joshua: Yes, Bob, I can. It is a process of daily practice. It is a process of, gradually, day-by-day, increasing your soul-strength. That is to say, of exercising the faculties which you already have, but in an unusual, or extraordinary, way. To do exercises, to practice awareness through self-reflection especially – that enables you to gain the strength to stay aware when your brain-mirror is no longer of use to you.

Bob: Is what we call meditation, or perhaps concentration, a key element in all this?

Joshua: Yes, it is. You have hit the nail on the head, so to speak. It is a training in learning to meditate, and to focus your attention on the subject of your meditation. This is the main thing for you to do in order to step across the threshold, and to be awake and aware of your new surroundings.

Bob: Joshua, are there specific meditations, or forms of meditation, which you and the other guides would recommend for this purpose?

Joshua: Yes, there are, and they will form the subject for the next chapter of this book.

Bob: In that case I suggest we stop for now and then turn to this theme in the next chapter. Do you agree?

Joshua: Yes, Bob, we do. Let us then go into more specific advice about what you or anyone else can do, if you choose to, in order to cross the threshold safely and consciously.

All blessings, Joshua Isaiah

4.
THE INNER PATH OF MEDITATION

Prologue

Bob: Joshua, I would like to see if one of the guides would like to come through to give the teaching for this chapter. What do you think?

Joshua: Shalom, my friend. Yes, Raja Lampa would love to work with you now and give his teachings.

Bob: Right.

Teaching

Raja: Yes, my friend, it is indeed a privilege to be able to once more work with you and to give advice which may be of assistance, to your readers especially.

Now, let us straight away talk about the 'inner path of meditations'. There are of course a plethora of meditations, as you know; many meditations and many meditation techniques. But why should we turn to this subject altogether? We turn to it because it provides the means whereby the human soul can strengthen itself to cross the threshold between the material and the spirit worlds, safely and surely. Meditation is the way in which those who are serious to make this crossing-over, can train themselves to remain awake and alert to the new reality in which they find themselves.

24

Now, straight away we are confronted by the challenge: 'How and what should we do meditatively in order to facilitate this step?' 'What meditation or meditations will work best for us, and how should we best go about doing them?' These are key questions. To some extent each person will need to solve these questions for themselves. It is a very individual matter. Nonetheless, clear guidance and advice can be given as to how to proceed. This is as follows. In the first place, it is a question of entering into the right mood and frame of mind. You cannot force your way into the spirit worlds. You must approach this task with due humility and sincerity. Also, you must ask yourself: 'Why altogether do I want to do this? What am I hoping to gain from it? What do I want to achieve?' In this way it is necessary to prepare yourselves in an honest and transparent way. If you have ulterior motives which are selfish in nature, then it is best to uncover these from the start. Be honest with yourself. That is the first requirement. If, after sufficient self-reflection, you have convinced yourself that your motive is a good one, by that I mean a motive for the greatest good of all concerned, then you are ready to take up a specific meditation content. We will give you a concrete example of this.

Imagine that you stand before a door. The door looks solid and impenetrable. It is heavy and dark. And yet it can be opened for you. There is one who stands on the other side of that heavy door who will open it for you, if you approach it rightly. My friends, you know the biblical saying: 'Knock and the door will be opened.' Well, this saying applies in this imagination – this meditation. You should hold in yourselves the feeling that if you are found worthy, then you may knock three times, and the door will be opened for you. You cannot open this heavy, solid door for yourself. You can only ask for your entry to be permitted. Now, my friends, if again and again you live with this inner meditation, if you hold this image again and again vividly in your mind and heart, then one day the door will open and you will be permitted to step through. You will then be making the first steps to explore the world beyond the door for yourself. Again, every step you take should be accompanied by the right mood and feeling, the feeling that you have been found worthy to go thus far. It is a feeling of thankfulness, a feeling of gratitude, a feeling of upliftment, which you should let resonate within your heart and soul. So, my friends, this is a concrete example of a meditation which can enable you to step over the threshold.

Now, we are not saying that this meditation will work for you the very first time that you try it. That is rather – indeed very – unlikely, unless of course you have already reached the necessary maturity of soul, perhaps through your previous lives on Earth. Such a thing is possible. However, for most of you it will be a matter of perseverance and practice; of again and again letting this picture, together with the appropriate feelings, live within you. However long it takes, you should know that when you are deemed ready by the powers that watch over you, you will succeed in your quest. Your wish will be granted you.

So you see, my friends, it really does come down to your own sincerity and perseverance. The one who guards the door will only let you pass through when he sees that you are ready for this step. He is there to protect you and see that you remain safe. He is not there to prevent you from entering when you yourself are ready to do so. But he knows that if you rush by heedlessly, you will do yourself great harm. He is there precisely to ensure your safety and health of mind, body and spirit. So, please look upon him as your friend, not your enemy! It is thanks to him that you will be allowed to wake up into the realm that in ordinary, daily life is closed to your awareness. Now, what I have described so far is simply the very beginning of your journey. It is, so to speak, the very first step. Once you have made this step safely, and also know how to safely step back again into your ordinary life, then you will be allowed to gradually, step-by-step, continue with your journey.

So, my friends, this is the teaching which I can give to you for this chapter. In succeeding chapters of the book, we as guides will show you how to proceed further on your journey into spirit worlds.

All blessings, Raja Lampa

Questions

Bob: Joshua, I would like now to ask some questions about the teaching that Raja Lampa has given. Is that alright?

Joshua: Shalom, my friend. Yes indeed, it is alright. Ask your questions and see who will step forward to answer them for you.

Bob: Right. So, my first question is this: Why in the meditation on the door should we knock three times? Isn't once enough!?

Pierre: I would like to step in here, please. The thrice times knocking, which Raja Lampa described to you, accords with a certain spiritual law: the Law of Three. It is a law which has been known throughout the ages. Yes, you may perhaps describe it as an arcane ritual, as something which is rooted deep in antiquity – but however you look at it, it constitutes a spiritual reality. So, this is the reason why you need to knock on the door – the heavy, impenetrable door that separates you from the spirit worlds – three times, and not just once.

Bob: Thank you, Pierre. The next question, please. Am I right in thinking that in doing this 'Door Meditation', shall I say, that we should try to hold this image as vividly as we can before our inner eye – our mind's eye – and also have the feelings, the expectations, which Raja pointed to? Is this the way to do it?

Pierre: Yes, my friend, it is. As you say, envision it as clearly as you can and know that this is the door which separates you, at present, from the realm of spirit. Then, with the right feelings in your heart and mind, walk up to the door and knock upon it three times, and then wait. Do not imagine that the door will automatically open, simply because you have knocked upon it. Be ready to wait for as long as it takes until the door is opened for you. You cannot open it yourself. There is no handle for you to turn which will open the door. It has to be opened to you from the other side. This is where the Watcher, or call him the Guardian of the Door, waits to see if you are ready to pass through. He will only open it when he sees that you have done the necessary work on yourself, to be fit and ready to gain entrance. This is for your own good. Again, it follows age-old laws of the spirit; laws for your own protection.

Bob: Yes, I understand this. Again, quite practically, when would you say is the best time to do this meditation? Morning or evening, for example. What would be most effective and appropriate?

Pierre: Well, this all depends on when you can best have the right feelings and attitudes towards this task. These feelings are the key things, so to speak. If you cannot summon up the right feelings, then the image by itself will not produce the desired results. In all such meditative work – inner work – the feelings and attitudes you have are all important.

Bob: So, could this be, for example, a morning meditation, or any time during the day for that matter, rather than at bedtime?

Pierre: Yes, certainly. If your attitudes are appropriate, then it can take place at any time of your choosing.

Bob: Right. Another practical question: How long should we allow to do such a meditation? Five minutes, five hours, or what?

Pierre: It is not a time factor so much as a quality factor. By this I mean, your ability to enter into the exercise in the right – the best – way. The time factor is then secondary, but obviously you have to gear yourselves to the practical situations of your life. You can't spend hours doing your inner work if you are needed to be somewhere else at a particular time.

Bob: Yes, very true. I didn't really envisage spending hours on such a task, but said this to illustrate my point!

Pierre: Yes, we realize that. However, the real point is to spend as long in the meditative state as feels right for you, as well as how it fits in with your outer obligations.

Bob: Understood. Another question: When eventually the door is opened, is that when we should step forward, so to speak, and walk through the doorway?

Pierre: Yes, it is. When you have been invited to enter, that is the right time to make this step in your meditation.

Bob: Right, and what then? Is it just a stepping into a realm of light, or how is that?

Pierre: It is a stepping into a realm of being; of being and sensing yourself as being in a quite different space, a quite different dimension.

Bob: Is this a joyful experience or a sombre one, or what?

Pierre: Well, my friend, since it is an experience which you have been waiting for and working towards, it is clearly an uplifting and joyful experience for you. You have been found ready to enter consciously, and safely, into a new realm of experience. A new land, so to speak.

Bob: Do we meet anyone there? Is there someone ready to greet us, to welcome us on the other side of the door?

Pierre: Yes, there is. In the first place it will be the Watcher, the Guardian, who will welcome you. He is the one who is your protector – the one who has your welfare at heart. So, he is the first person – rather, the being – who you will meet on the spirit side of life.

Bob: And how will we recognize him as such?

Pierre: He recognizes you, and because of this you will also know him as the one who is assigned to take care of you. It is a knowledge which you have, simply because you have gained access to this realm of being. When you see him, you will know him.

Bob: Right, Pierre, is there anything else which you feel we should know or be aware of?

Pierre: The most important thing is to be aware of your own motives for seeking to cross the threshold between the worlds. Be true to yourself; know, as clearly as you possibly can, why you are doing this. Your motives need to be pure, in the sense that they are not selfish or intended to take advantage of others for your own ends. This is the most important point to be crystal clear about. If this is clear to you, then all else follows on in due course. Patience here is the key.

All blessings, Pierre

Bob: Thank you. Joshua do you have a title for the next chapter already?

Joshua: Yes we do. Let's call it: 'Further Explorations beyond the Door'.

Postscript:

There are clearly two aspects to the 'Door Meditation'. On the one hand, it is a meditative visualization exercise. In this exercise we can, at a certain point, see or picture the door being opened for us. However, there is also the actual spiritual reality that occurs, when we are then permitted to really cross over this threshold between the worlds.

So, in this sense the opening of the door takes place on two levels. Firstly, in our own visualized scenario, and then, secondly, in spirit actuality. This same sort of differentiation is applicable to the other meditations that will also be described in the course of our spiritual progression.

5.
FURTHER EXPLORATIONS
BEYOND THE 'DOOR'

Prologue

Bob: Joshua, I am again ready to work with the guides in order to explore further how to enter the spirit worlds consciously and safely. Are you and they ready to help me in this?

Joshua: Shalom, my friend. Yes, we are. Let us see how we shall proceed today, and who would like to give you teachings.

Bob: Right. I think Markos wishes to step forward, am I right?

Joshua: Shalom, my friend. Yes, you are.

Teaching

Markos: So, my friend, let us see how we shall move forward on this journey – this spiritual journey, we can say. So, we have come to the point that, through the use of the 'Door Meditation', entrance into the spirit world or worlds has been permitted by the Watcher, the Guardian. That is the one, the being, who has responsibility for ensuring that the seeker only crosses over – between the worlds – when the necessary degree of maturity has been attained. The question now is: 'How to proceed to journey further, beyond this point?' The teaching which

I will give you today is designed to give you a clear picture of the next steps on your journey.

So, in the first instance, let us acknowledge once again that it is through the strengthening of the soul, through meditative exercises and practice, that the way into spirit worlds is gained. Meditation, that is to say, immersion in certain specific contents, inner contents, is the way, the method, whereby your journey is to be effected. You therefore wonder, my friend, and rightly so, what other meditative contents do you need in order to continue with your adventure? I will give you such contents today. The 'Door Meditation', as we have called it, is the first such content. However, once the threshold has been crossed successfully, you need another meditation to steer you along the right course. By right course I mean to say, the course, the direction, which leads you step-by-step into different regions of the spirit worlds. The spirit worlds are multifaceted and multilayered, we could say. Just as in the physical, material world you have many differentiations, many places to go and see, many different areas of the world to explore and to familiarize yourself with, so similarly in the spirit worlds there are many areas, regions, parts, to discover for yourself. But remember, my friend, that whereas in the physical world you are exploring physical regions, countries, etc., in the spirit worlds it is a question of meeting different beings. This spirit world is a world of beings – beings standing at all different levels of consciousness, of evolution and development. So, my friend, your way forward is by getting to know the different beings who live in the spirit worlds, and this is what your meditations will guide you towards.

Let me now be quite concrete and specific in what I will say next. The next meditation which we would like to give you is the following.

Imagine that you are now standing on the other side of the threshold, having stepped through 'the doorway'. You are now met by a specific being. This is your angel. It is that same being, that spiritual being, who has accompanied you through all your incarnations on Earth. This being is intimately connected to you. This being has the task to lead you on through all cycles of time to find your own true self. This is the task of your angel – to guide you to know and meet yourself. So now in this meditation, let us call it the 'Angel Meditation', you should imagine being greeted, welcomed, by your angel on the far side of the threshold. Your angel will take you by the hand and will gently lead you along a pathway. Go with your angel. Put your entire trust in your angel to guide you safely and surely along the path ahead. This is what you need to do in your meditation. Go along with the angel and see where you will be led. It is a meditation of trust; it is a meditation in which you feel that your brother or sister in spirit is now guiding you along the way. Where you will come to, you must wait and see. However, we can already tell you that you will be guided to the inner Temple, the inner Sanctuary, in which you will meet other beings, other guides, who will lead you further along your way.

However, it is sufficient for today if we stop here, having provided you with the next imagination for your meditative work, namely, what we have called, the 'Angel Meditation'.

All blessings, Markos

Questions

Bob: Joshua I am ready to carry on today working with the guides on this journey into spirit worlds and, no doubt, the path to discover one's own true or higher Self. Since the last teachings have given us the 'Angel Meditation', I think it makes sense to direct the questions I have to Philip, as my guardian angel. Do you agree with this, Joshua?

Joshua: Shalom, my friend. Yes, I entirely agree with what you propose. Philip stands ready to answer your questions today.

Bob: Right. So, Philip, my first question is this: 'Do you agree with the teachings which Markos gave and his description of the so-called 'Angel Meditation'?

Philip: Yes, my friend and brother, I do. Markos has given sound and true teachings which are designed to enable the seeker after truth to continue the journey into spirit worlds beyond the threshold.

Bob: Very well, Philip. I would like to ask concrete questions concerning this meditative task. 'How should we imagine this meeting with the angel; how should we best picture this in our inner life?'

Philip: My friend and brother, you should, we suggest, simply picture this as you would if you were meeting an old friend; someone who you have known for a long time and whom you trust. You don't need to imagine some figure in a thin veil, a flowing veil, shall we say. Some supernatural being. No, keep your picture more matter-of-fact. Simply imagine, and feel, that you are welcomed by a good and trusted friend. This friend then takes you by the hand, and leads you gently along the path which stretches ahead. Walk with your friend along this pathway.

Bob: Right. But how should, or could, we imagine this pathway. After all, there are lots of ways to imagine a path, aren't there? It could be like a country lane, it could be a path near a road, it could be a track along the cliff-tops overlooking the sea, etc. In other words, we could envision any number of pathways. So, how do we best go about this?

Philip: Simply see what arises in your mind, in your soul, in your imagination. Just let it come to you, without preconceptions of how you think it should look. Instead of trying to construct something, just let the picture, for you, emerge – let it appear for your inner eye, so to speak. Remember, the meditation is an Imagination, that is to say, a pictorial process. The main thing is, don't try to force anything. Remember you are being helped and guided. So go with the flow.

Bob: So, are you saying with this, Philip, that the picture could be different for each person? That it is very individual how this can be seen or expressed?

Philip: Precisely, my friend and brother. It is entirely individual, but nonetheless it embraces the same basic theme. You are being led further along the pathway into the spirit worlds.

Bob: Markos indicated that this way leads towards a sort of 'inner Temple', we could say, a sort of sanctuary in which we shall receive further guidance. Is that correct?

Philip: It is correct. Yes, there are 'temples', 'sanctuaries', in spirit worlds. That is to say, places, centres, locations, where higher spirit beings are waiting to help you further on your journey. Remember, my friend and brother, you are watched over with each step you take. The higher beings are full of care for your safety and welfare, and they also acknowledge the courageous steps which you are making.

Bob: Why do you say 'courageous steps'?

Philip: Because it does require courage to step out of your normal, down-to-earth, comfort zone, and to start to explore quite new dimensions of experience and reality.

Bob: Well, yes I can see this. Though I've actually still to do it!

Philip: Yes that is true, but that is precisely why you are working with us now. To discover the way in which these things, this adventure, we could say, can be achieved, can be done.

Bob: Yes, that is so. One final question, Philip. 'Can we be sure that this way is safe – I mean that we don't fall into traps of illusion; or, perhaps, be deliberately misled?'

Philip: It is a safe way because as guides we have your – and by your I mean this to refer to each human being who is seriously seeking – we have your welfare at heart. Remember, we also serve Divine Laws. We follow, as it were, instructions from higher beings who are full of Wisdom and Love. Above all, we are servants of the all Divine Purpose and Creator of the Universe, the Universal All.

Bob: Well, that's quite a lot to take in – for me at least!

Philip: Yes it is, but it is important for you to realize that there is nothing arbitrary about what we are doing with you. It is sanctioned and protected by higher sources of Wisdom and Love. Ultimately, by the Divine that permeates all being.

All blessings, Philip

Bob: Joshua, I have no idea what theme, title, heading, the next chapter should have. Can you supply me with this already, or do I need to wait for it?

Joshua: I can give you this title. Let us call it 'Standing within the Temple'.

All blessings, Joshua Isaiah

Bob: Right, thank you. I will resume tomorrow morning.

*

Bob: Joshua, at this point, and before going on to Chapter 6, I would like to ask further questions of you and the other guides about what we are doing. Is this alright?

Joshua: Shalom, my friend. Yes of course, this is perfectly alright with us.

Bob: So, my questions are essentially ones of clarification and transparency, so that I and my readers are quite clear what this book is about. Am I right in saying that the route which is being described and laid out here is open for all to walk if they so choose?

Joshua: Yes, you are. It is a path which is accessible to all who wish to enter into spirit worlds, safely and consciously.

Bob: Does this mean that there are no dangers or pitfalls to be met on this path?

Markos: No pitfalls, provided the right preparations are done beforehand, and that patience and perseverance are present on behalf of the seeker.

Bob: But Rudolf Steiner in his teachings, with which I am familiar, does emphasize that there are tempting beings, shall we say, that can lead a seeker astray. Isn't that so?

Markos: Yes, it is so, if the right precautions are not taken. However, we have said already that everything depends upon the correct strengthening of the soul-forces prior to undertaking this journey.

Bob: I understand that, and certainly Steiner says the same. But what other safeguards are there, to give the seeker confidence and reassurance?

Markos: Well, my friend, remember that you will not be making a step over the threshold until the door has been opened. The door will only be opened when you are seen to be ready to proceed.

Bob: So, is that Watcher at the gate, or door – that Guardian – the safeguard to our entry?

Markos: Absolutely. If he sees you are not sufficiently prepared, you will not gain entrance, however hard you try.

Bob: Yes, I understand that. But this means we, or I, could be waiting a very long time!

Red Cloud: Yes, it does, but it is for your own good. Those who are hasty and impatient cannot be granted safe passage.

Bob: So in that case would it just be a question, shall I say, of persevering with the 'Door Meditation' until it can actually be opened?

Red Cloud: Precisely. This is where the patience and perseverance comes in. Those who are prepared to wait until they have been proved ready, will then eventually achieve the goal they seek.

Bob: Right. So, to state the obvious, it really is a serious undertaking to seek such entry into the spirit worlds?

Red Cloud: It is indeed. It is not a light matter, but, if you really do seek true knowledge of who you really are, in your spiritual essence, then this is the way to go.

Bob: Another question. We live in a time, in an age, when there are lots and lots of spiritual paths, you might say. Lots of choice and diversity. So, how should a person know which way he or she can really trust and feel is authentic?

Raja: Well, what you say is indeed true. There is much choice and, in a sense, each person must discover their own way. Just as each person has to walk their own pathway through earthly life, to follow their own destiny, so it is also in the spiritual life, the inner life, we can say.

Bob: Yes, this is understandable. But aren't there more reliable ways to go, shall we say, whereas others are more questionable?

Raja: Yes, that is also true. To an extent it depends on the culture and the background which a person is comfortable with, in that it forms their beliefs and traditions. However, it is also a matter of seeing what speaks true for each individual case. What speaks to your own heart and mind.

Bob: Well, yes, that is fine – but, for example, Steiner maintained that there were certain ways that were outmoded for modern people, which were alright for earlier times. Was he correct in this?

Raja: Yes, he was correct in saying this, but even so, he would still maintain that each person has to find a way that accords with their own destiny and karma.

Bob: Yes, that may well be true. My purpose in writing this book is really to present a way into spirit worlds that is accessible to 'ordinary' people. By this I mean people who are seriously searching to find answers to life's questions, and who feel that they need to journey into spirit worlds themselves to do this. Does this make sense to you?

Raja: It makes perfect sense to us, which is, of course, the reason why we are so willing to work with you on this. So, well done for this, my friend.

Bob: One more question. Isn't it necessary to learn how to leave our physical bodies consciously and safely, at will, and that this is the key to gaining access to spirit realms?

Raja: Yes, it is. You are effectively needing to do what you do, unconsciously, every time you fall asleep. To go out of yourselves. But, through inner training, you want to acquire this ability consciously and with awareness.

Bob: And the way to do this is by practising the meditations?

Raja: Exactly. This is the way to achieve your goal and lift your consciousness out of the physical sheath.

Bob: But then, how do we make sure we do this safely, and get back in properly?

Raja: Well, it is a matter of practice. As you get better at doing your meditations, you will have the feeling that all is going well, and that you can achieve to do this.

Bob: But couldn't it be rather scary?

Raja: It could, but it doesn't need to be. This is where trust comes in. If your motives are sound and you do things for the right reasons, then the safeguards are more or less automatically in place.

Bob: So, we need to be very clear about why, and for what reasons, we want to tread this path?

Raja: You do indeed. It must be for the greatest good of all involved.

Bob: So not just some form of escapism from ordinary life?

Red Cloud: No, indeed, it needs to be for the good of the whole world that you seek higher knowledge and certainty.

Bob: I think this is the note to end this questioning on. Do you agree?

Red Cloud: We do indeed. It is the right note to always have well in mind.

Bob: Many thanks.

6.
STANDING WITHIN THE TEMPLE

Prologue

Bob: Joshua, I am now ready again to work with the guides and I just had the name 'Isobel' in my mind. Could it be that Isobel wishes to give the teaching for this chapter, or does another guide wish to come through?

Joshua: Shalom, my friend. Yes, you are right, it is Isobel who wishes to step forward for this chapter.

Bob: Right, then please go ahead, Isobel, and I will write what you give me.

Teaching

Isobel: Thank you, my friend. Yes, I have not previously worked with you, in the sense that the other guides who you know have done so. Nonetheless, I am grateful for the opportunity to do so now. So, my friend, we will now turn to the theme of this chapter, namely, 'Standing Within the Temple', and see where this will lead us.

Just to recap, the teachings which you have received so far are designed to guide you and others along a route into spirit worlds and to do so in full consciousness. This is the task which you gave yourself when you envisaged this new book, and it is a task which we are happy to help you with. You, we, have now come so far that the angel assigned to each person, each individual,

43

has led you to the Temple. That is to say, to that place in spirit where you can meet higher guides, we could say. That is, spirit beings who have the wish to help you further, as a seeker for Truth and for Knowledge. These beings belong to the ranks of the angelic hierarchies; higher beings than the angels *per se*, but we can think of them as 'angelic hierarchies', in order to give them a name which readers can relate to, hopefully!

So, what happens when you reach the Temple, the Sanctuary, the place of blessedness – we could say, a 'sacred space'? There, important meetings and conversations can take place. Here we would ask you to place before yourselves another pictorial meditation as an Imagination. Imagine my friends that, with your angel, you have entered into the Temple which you can visualize as a rounded, domed building – a domed building rather than anything too church-like, shall we say. Now, you can walk along this building until you come to a resting place. It is not an altar but rather a place where you can sit down quietly and await whoever will come to meet you here. Your angel can also stand beside you, but he also simply waits to see who will be the first to greet you and welcome you into this sacred space. You sit there in quiet expectation, open to receive whoever will appear to you. It is a holy space, in that you can feel a sense of awe and wonder and reverence, we can say, for being allowed to sit there. Eventually, you will feel, or perhaps even see, a friend appear with you. This is a being from the higher hierarchies, we could say. We do not need to specify from which hierarchy or grouping this being has come. The important thing is that you know he is there to be of help and service to you on your quest for Truth and Knowledge. You are asked simply to be open to whatever will pass between you. He will, in fact, guide you on to the next stage of your journey, and will also reveal to you the nature of the worlds in which you are moving. In other words, through this higher being, this representative of the Divine Will, you will become aware of how far you have come so far, and also the direction of your further travels. For this guidance and knowledge you feel a certain humility and thankfulness.

This then is the meditation, we can call it the inner 'Temple Meditation' perhaps, in order for you to identify yourself with it in your meditative life. So this, my friend, is how far you have come on your journey to know the spirit worlds.

All blessings, Isobel

Questions

Bob: Today, Joshua, I will follow up this teaching straight away with some questions please. Is that alright?

Joshua: Shalom, my friend. Yes, of course, this is alright with us. Simply ask what you need to know or to clarify. All blessings, Joshua.

Bob: Right. Now, I am wondering how I will be learning about, or experiencing, spirit worlds consciously by sinking myself, so to speak, in such meditations as the guides are giving me? How does that work? Are the meditations like doorways, or portals, through which I enter into these new dimensions, or how is that please?

Isobel: Let me step forward to answer your questions. Yes, you have a correct conception of what these meditations can do for you if you think of them as opening-up doors, or windows perhaps, into the higher dimensions of existence. It is precisely through entering into these different meditations that you will progress through the spheres, or levels, of the spirit worlds. We can only give you the tools, the methods, which you can freely take up if you wish to do so. You will then discover for yourself how these tools work. You will have your own experiences in these new dimensions.

Bob: Right, Isobel. I can go with that, in the sense that it is only if I use these tools, these meditative contents, that I will find out what vistas they open up for me. Is that right?

Isobel: Yes, that is correct, my friend. You will find that, through your inner efforts, your inner work, you will be led onwards into ever widening realms of experience. Now, we cannot tell you how that is, because, until you make your own experiences, it would be meaningless for you. It is like describing the scenery on a journey which is quite unlike anything you have previously experienced. Only through the new experiences does it become a reality for you.

Bob: Yes, I can accept that. But a key question for me is: 'Are we – am I – being guided safely and surely along this new way, if I work sincerely with the contents you and the other guides are giving?'

Isobel: Yes, you are, provided of course that you trust in the process. Trust is the key word here, because you are being tested, you could say, in the degree of trust which you bring to this endeavour.

Bob: Right, but surely this can't just be blind trust?

Isobel: No, it cannot. It is a trust that grows with each step that you take, because you have the clear feeling this is leading you rightly into these worlds.

Bob: So, it really is a process of growth, of growing into the new worlds of experience. Is that right?

Isobel: Yes it is, and that is a good way of expressing it. You grow through your experiences.

Bob: But can I, for example, decide at any point on this journey that I do not wish to proceed; that I can turn back and say, that is enough, for now at least?

Isobel: Yes, you can. Your free will is in no way compromised. At any point, you can decide to stop the journey and turn back.

Bob: What I mean with this is that the whole purpose of this journey, this exploration into spirit realms, needs to be clear to me, doesn't it?

Isobel: Yes, it does. The purpose is of course to be able to take your place as a person of knowledge, in the whole world process. In other words, through your expanded knowledge, especially of yourself, to become a better, more complete human being, and thereby to help your fellow men and women. This is the purpose of any true seeking for knowledge, whether on the earthly plane itself or on higher planes of existence. Do you agree with me on this?

Bob: Yes, I do. My understanding is that the so-called initiates are there to help all human beings to achieve their own true goals, and to further the course of evolution.

Isobel: Yes, Bob, you are right in this. This has always been the goal of all those advanced human beings who wish to serve mankind.

Bob: So, Isobel, I think I've noted all the questions I need to for this morning. Thank you.

Isobel: Thank you, my friend, and all blessings on your efforts on behalf of humanity.

Bob: Actually, Joshua, there is of course just one more question. What is the title for the next chapter – can you tell me this already?

Joshua: Yes, I can, Bob. The title we will give it is, 'Further Work on the Pathway'.

Bob: Right. Thank you.

7.
FURTHER WORK ON THE PATHWAY

Prologue

Bob: Joshua, I now wish to link in with you and the other guides to pursue the subject of this book, namely: 'Journeying into Spirit Worlds, Safely and Consciously'. Is this alright for everyone?

Joshua: Shalom, my friend. Yes it is, we stand ready to help you with this task.

Bob: Right. I wonder who wishes to step forward to give the teaching today?

Gopi Ananda: May I do so, my friend? This will be the first time we have worked together in this way.

Bob: Yes indeed, Gopi, I look forward to what you will bring.

Teaching

Gopi Ananda: So, my friend, although you have been aware of me for some time, it is only now that we work together in this way. I will give you teachings which follow on and continue what you have received so far.

Let us proceed from the situation in which you found yourself when you had been guided to the Temple. In that sacred space you met other beings – beings of the higher worlds, we can say. These beings had the task to make you aware that you are on a journey to come to your own true self, your spirit Self. In order to fulfil this task, this journey will lead you further into higher and higher regions of the spirit worlds. There you will meet exalted beings. I mean by this, beings who stand far above the present evolutionary level of human beings, at least with very few exceptions. The exceptions will be those human beings who have already attained a very high level of development, the so-called initiates. However, for the vast majority of human beings – of human souls – this level of being is far above them at present. So, my friend, you are to be made aware on your onward journey of these high, exalted beings. In order to help you to do this, we will give you another meditation – another meditative exercise to work at. It is as follows.

Imagine yourself standing on a high mountain from which you can survey the terrain below. Imagine this mountain as covered by pure, white snow. There is no blemish, no dirtiness shall we say, but just a beautiful, pristine, pure white surface. Next, imagine that you turn your gaze towards the starry heavens – the star-studded sky. You see a multitude of shining points of light and, as you gaze towards them, you feel yourself travelling out from your body in order to reach the stars. The stars are inviting you to come to them; the beings who reside in the stars – or, shall we say, behind the images of the stars – are inviting you to join them. This is therefore the task of this meditation – let us call it the 'Stars Meditation' – for you to let go of your normal consciousness and to travel to the regions of the stars; to join the beings who wait for you there. Do this, my friend, in quiet, inward meditation. In the quiet of your room, journey outwards in your consciousness to the starry realm, knowing that there you will meet divine beings – beings of the higher hierarchies – beings who oversee the working of the whole universe. This is the task which, if you work at it patiently, will enable you to feel in the presence of exalted beings. Amongst these beings, my friend, you will also discover your own true I, your own true being whom you have heard of in your studies, but never before met consciously. In the starry realm you will be able to find yourself! This is the challenge which awaits you on this journey into the spirit worlds.

All blessings, Gopi Ananda

Questions

Bob: Well, Joshua, in a moment I will straightaway ask some questions concerning this last teaching. Is that alright?

Joshua: Shalom, my friend. Of course this is alright. We expect you to ask the questions which you need to in order to clarify this teaching.

Bob: So, Joshua, I've had a break and now will ask some questions. First, am I right in thinking that I have, so to speak, left 'the Temple' and now find myself on the mountain top?

Gopi: Let me step forward my friend to clarify things for you as far as I can. Yes, you are correct in making this next, new step on your journey. You move from the Temple situation to the heights of the mountain. This is your springboard, so to speak, for your journey to the stars.

Bob: And the pureness of the mountain top – the white, pristine, pure snow – is this also symbolic of how I should try to feel inside myself?

Gopi: Yes, precisely. You try to imagine yourself in this pure state of being. You try to put behind you, or below you, all impure thoughts, or feelings, or wishes, and see yourself supported by the inner strength of this pure and beautiful landscape. You stand on the heights, ready to stretch out and reach higher in your consciousness.

Bob: So, to really imagine I am almost flying upwards to the stars? Not exactly like a rocket, shall I say, but nonetheless travelling into those starry spaces of the universe?

Gopi: Yes, that is correct – but 'behind' the stars, so to speak, you find the beings who are ready to greet you. The stars as such are not your goal, but the beings who stand behind them.

Bob: And will I know, or sense, or feel, the presence of these beings?

Gopi: Yes, you will, provided that you enter there with a pure heart and mind, or at the least, as pure as you can attain at this stage in your journey. Remember, my friend, we know you are a striving soul, not a perfect soul, since hardly anyone is. The important thing is your clear intention and your motivation for this work.

Bob: Which is?

Gopi: Which is, my friend, that you wish to connect with your true Self and, in doing so, to become a more conscious and helpful member of humanity. This is the goal which you set yourself.

Bob: But I am certainly anything but pure! I am very aware, painfully so, of many blemishes and shortcomings in my personality and character.

Gopi: We are not expecting you to be as pure as the driven snow! We only expect you to try your best to raise your consciousness towards the goal you seek, in the right spirit of humility, reverence and compassion.

Bob: Compassion for who?

Gopi: Well, for yourself, as well as for the rest of your fellow human beings.

Bob: Perhaps in the sense that the Buddha showed and felt compassion for all sentient beings?

Gopi: Yes, precisely so. A compassion that encompasses the whole of creation – of the created and manifest world.

Bob: So, just to summarize. It is a question of doing one's best, but with a clear knowledge of one's intentions, aims and motivations. Is that right?

Gopi: Yes, that is right. This is, after all, all that you can do. And remember, you may not succeed in your exercises, your meditations, the first time! It may require much perseverance for you to achieve the goals you seek, but know that higher beings are watching over you and applauding your sincere efforts.

Bob: I think that's a very positive note to end on. Do you agree?

Gopi: We all agree.

All blessings, my friend. Gopi Ananda

Bob: Actually, Joshua, do you know the title or theme of the next chapter already please?

Joshua: Yes, please call it: 'Cosmic Consciousness'.

All blessings, Joshua

8.
COSMIC CONSCIOUSNESS

Prologue

Bob: Well, Joshua, here I am again and ready to see what will be given today. Are the guides also ready?
Joshua: Shalom, my friend. Yes we are. We are keen to help you further on this new project.
Bob: Right. So, who wishes to give the teaching today, I wonder? Which guide will now step forward?
Pierre: I would like to do so, my friend. I will give the teaching today.

Teaching

Pierre: Now, you have come a long way, quite far we would say, in your journey into spirit worlds. You have now reached the point where you can enter, meditatively, into an experience of being at one with All That Is. This is what is meant by the term 'cosmic consciousness'. It means that you enter into that state of awareness or consciousness where all separation drops away from you. Yes, you still retain a sense of your own being, but your being is completely merged and at one with *All That Is*. You feel completely at one with the universal all – or you could say, you feel at one with God. It is, we could say, a 'God-consciousness' that you now experience, and you feel both supported and immersed within the totality of this experience.

In order for you to enter this state consciously, we will now give you the following meditation, again in picture form. Imagine, my friend, that you have been in the starry heavens, so to speak. You have dwelt with the beings of the stars. Now, as a further step along your path, you move beyond the stars. You enter into a space, into a void, which lies further away, beyond the realm of the fixed stars. You now enter into the creative space of the Being who oversees the whole manifest universe. This Being, this divine universal being who is the creative source of All That Is, stands behind the starry worlds. He (though 'He' is only figurative) is the Being through whom the entire cosmos has its origins. A Being so great, so powerful, that it is almost beyond your imagination or ability to conceive. Nonetheless, try to imagine that you have come close to this Being, the One who presides over all worlds. The One who knows and sees all worlds, both material and spiritual. Yes, the One who in Christian tradition is designated as 'the Father'. This is then the content of your meditation – to try to imagine yourself in this new situation. If you can achieve this, then you also know that you are a part of this one-ness; that you are identified in this state of consciousness with the Being who cares for the world as a Father cares for his son or his children. It is a feeling of immeasurable and limitless Love. This Being is nothing else but Love, in its purest and most encompassing form and quality. This is the only way we can describe this state to you. You feel totally upheld and cared for. The Universal Power of Love – this is the Father-God. So this, my friend, is the task for you to work on at this stage of your journey into spirit worlds. It is a sublime task and one which you will be able to achieve, if you have managed to achieve all the previous steps on your journey. When you reach this stage, you have come to the summit, the heights of your experience of the Divine Being. In a sense, you have achieved your goal to the fullest extent possible for a human being. And, in this experience, at this point, you also know yourself to be a member of the Godhead. You realize your own divine status as a spiritual being. You have achieved the self-knowledge which has been your goal from the start of your journey. So, this is the teaching which we wished to give you today.

All blessings, Pierre

Questions

Bob: Joshua, I would like to straight away ask some questions to do with this teaching. Is that alright?

Joshua: Shalom, my friend. Of course, that is alright. Simply ask and we will endeavour to give you the answers you are seeking.

Bob: Right. Well, I suppose the first question is: 'If one really does reach this level of awareness, this sublime state, isn't there a real danger of not wanting to return to normal, everyday life? How can one move from a state of universal-all, to be back into the day-to-day chores of life?'

Pierre: My friend, it is a good question. Yes, it may seem – having reached such a universal state of awareness – that normal, earthly existence seems far removed for you. However, that is not the case. In a sense, you carry something of that united feeling back with you, when you step out from your meditative state. You have a feeling of the universality of all existence – that everything is held together, you could say, by a universal power of Love. This Love should also find expression in your day-to-day life on Earth. Indeed, it is the essence – and what is essential – of the Christian tradition which you know of. Christ, as the divine Son-Being, or the Being of the Sun, brought this teaching through His example into earthly life. So, in a sense – a very real sense – this consciousness of divine all-encompassing Love is the very teaching which was given by the Christ more than 2,000 years ago. This is a teaching which is meant to illuminate and embrace all of earthly existence, including your day-to-day life. In a sense, again in a very real sense, it finds expression in the words: 'Not I, but Christ in me.' So, we could also say, that the meditative experience you have at this stage in your journey leads again back to earthly life which has been – is – permeated by the Christ-force; the force of Universal Love. We realize, my friend, that all this is a lot to take in. Nonetheless, this is the answer we can give you to your question.

All blessings, Pierre

Bob: Thank you, Pierre. So, are you also saying that it is important that the meditation enables one to come back into normal, everyday life with a renewed sense, shall I say, for the Love that actually permeates and upholds all existence? Is that correct?

Pierre: Absolutely correct, my friend. You now know, deep in your own heart, that it is the power of divine

Love which upholds you, and all that there is. This is the goal of your striving through the incarnations in earthly life, to realize this reality. It is a long-term goal, but it is also a goal which can be achieved through deep meditation.

Bob: Well, I didn't really expect this when I embarked on entering into spirit worlds!

Pierre: No, perhaps not. But the way we have described for you is an ever-ascending journey, into ever deeper spiritual levels of experience. It is both an exploration of spirit worlds as well as being an exploration of your own true being.

Bob: And does this experience of divine Love in cosmic consciousness, does this bring this journey to an end?

Pierre: To say 'an end' is not really correct. It is more of a movement, a cyclic movement, towards knowing who you are and what stands behind the manifest reality of the world. So, it brings you full circle, you might say, rather than coming to the end of the line. However, it is something which needs to be experienced, rather than just speculated upon.

Bob: So, would this then bring this book to a close? Is that how far we have come?

Pierre: Yes, that is true. With this you have received the contents and the teachings which will lead you on the path which initiated your impulse to write this book with us.

Bob: So, all that remains is to take up these teachings, these meditations, and endeavour to enter into these experiences. Is that right?

Pierre: Yes it is, but remember that both patience and per-severance are needed if you, or others, are really serious about this work. It is not something to be undertaken light-heartedly, in the sense of here today and gone tomorrow. It is a task which only you can set yourself, but then it is up to you to be true to the task also.

Bob: Well, yes. But are we quite free to stop, or pause, at any point on this journey, if we feel that is enough for now?

Pierre: You are. There is no compulsion whatsoever. It is a journey that can be made by a free spirit, so at any point you can decide to stop until you feel it is right for you to continue.

Bob: Well, that is reassuring, Pierre. Do you agree with me that it is essential that a person maintains their health in mind, body and spirit? After all, some of these experiences are quite mind-blowing, aren't they?

Pierre: Yes indeed, in this you are absolutely correct. Health of mind, body and spirit is a priority, and that is why you should continually train yourself to be in self-control, and to maintain a high level of personal integrity and ethical responsibility. These are ongoing prerequisites for your own safety and sanity. This is not a journey for the fainthearted, though ultimately it can become a journey for 'everyman', in the sense that it lies as the hidden potential within all human nature.

Bob: Well, Pierre, you and the other guides have certainly given much food for thought, and I will have to see where I take this from here. Many thanks.

Pierre: You are more than welcome. We send you our greetings and our blessings. Your friends in Spirit.

Bob: Joshua, I feel that one or two more chapters are needed, both to reflect on and summarize what has been given. Do you agree with me?

Joshua: Shalom, my friend. Yes, I do – and yes, we do. By all means continue to work with us. Ask whatever questions are important to you, and we will do our best to provide the answers you need. This is an important project and we are happy to cooperate with you.

Bob: As regards a title for the next chapter, I would suggest: 'Further Questions on the Way'. What do you think?

Joshua: Yes, Bob, a good choice of words, we would say. Let that be the title for the next chapter.

All blessings, Joshua

9.
FURTHER QUESTIONS ON THE WAY

Further questions

Bob: Joshua, I would like to begin with some questions about 'the Way' that's been described. Is that alright?

Joshua: Yes it is, my friend. We anticipate that you might have quite a number of questions on this theme.

Bob: Yes, and it's also a question of where to start! So, let me start with this. How long might this journey into spirit worlds take?

Joshua: Well, it will take as long as needs be for each person. It is entirely individual and therefore no time can be placed on it.

Bob: Well, yes, I anticipated that answer. However, are we talking weeks, months, years, or what?

Joshua: My friend, it can even take a lifetime! It really does depend on how each individual approaches the work that needs to be done, and, in addition, it depends on the powers-that-be seeing just how ready and prepared the person is.

Bob: So, Joshua, are you saying, or implying, that how far we get also depends on what the spiritual beings make of it? I mean, that they see whether we are ready for a certain step or not?

Joshua: Yes, my friend, that is exactly it, and this also provides the safeguard. No one wishes you to come to harm, to come to grief, and that is why careful surveillance, you could say, is made at each step.

Bob: Well, Joshua, that is on the one hand reassuring but, on the other hand, it makes me wonder how 'free' we are in pursuing this path?

Joshua: You are quite free but, on the other hand, you have certain responsibilities to yourself and to others. This is the reason why you are watched over, and also helped as needs be.

Bob: Right, another question. How important is it that we approach each of the meditations with the right feeling or mood?

Raja: It is absolutely essential that this is there. The right mood is almost more important than the right thoughts. Both are important, but the mood and attitude is paramount.

Bob: How would you describe the right mood for this work?

Raja: It is on the one hand one of humility, but on the other hand also a courageous attitude is called for. Just as the early explorers needed to have courage to undertake their voyages of discovery, so you, my friend, also need enough courage to enter into spirit worlds.

Bob: Why?

Raja: Because you enter into new dimensions for your experience, and you need to put your trust in the powers-that-be to see you safely along the way.

Bob: And who are the 'powers-that-be' that you refer to?

Raja: They are higher beings of the spirit world, who have the task to oversee your journey.

Bob: Does this include Philip, as my angel?

Raja: Yes it does, especially initially, but later along the route, higher – more knowledgeable – beings will be your guides.

Bob: So, is this different from you, Raja, and the other guides with whom I am in contact?

Raja: Yes, these are higher spirit guides. We – Joshua, John, etc. – are guides for you in the sense that we can point the way, and are also permitted to give you the appropriate tools, the meditations, but it is on higher beings to actually lead and guide you along the way.

Bob: Are we here talking about the beings that belong, shall we say, to the 'higher hierarchies', as Rudolf Steiner referred to them?

Raja: Precisely so. It is such beings that we are referring to also.

Bob: In my previous book, you and my other guides gave me descriptions of the spirit worlds, whereas this present book has much more to do with making our own experiences. Will the meditations open doors, so to speak, into different levels and regions of the spirit worlds?

Raja: Yes, they will.

Bob: And will we then meet beings – say, deceased human beings, as well as purely spiritual beings?

Raja: Yes, you will.

Bob: But will we be able to recognize, to discern, who is who?

Raja: Well, you will be helped and guided in this and introduced, shall I say, to whom you are interrelating with.

Bob: Will this also ensure our wellbeing and safe-keeping?

Raja: Yes, provided you heed the guidance and advice which you receive. Even here, you still have free will, and so you need to tread carefully.

Bob: So, maybe this is where the courage also comes in?

Raja: Indeed it does. However, let us reassure you that you are still being watched over and, in that sense, protected step-by-step.

Bob: Thank you. I'll stop this session for now and resume later.

Raja: Good. All blessings.

*

Bob: Joshua, I would like to continue to ask questions concerning the Path or Way that the guides have described, whereby to enter consciously and safely into the spirit worlds. Is this alright?

Joshua: Shalom, my friend. Yes, it is indeed alright for you to do so. So, please proceed to ask your questions.

Bob: Right. Through my knowledge of Rudolf Steiner's teachings I am aware that he says that on the way, or journey, into spirit worlds we will also encounter beings, spiritual beings, who endeavour to distract or mislead human beings. He calls these the 'luciferic' and 'ahrimanic' beings. Do you know what he is talking about?

Joshua: Yes, we do, and he is quite correct to point to their influences on human beings – especially those who are seeking to know the Truth.

Bob: Well, in that case if we (I and our readers) engage in the meditative pathway which the guides have given us, do we also need to be aware of such beings or not?

Joshua: Yes, you do, but remember, on the path that we have described you are constantly being watched over and led safely forwards and upwards.

Bob: Yes, but does that mean that we are not subject to these opposing beings, if I describe them like that?

64

Joshua: Well, you will have experiences on the path and you will become aware of beings, because the spirit worlds are worlds of beings, rather than things. So yes, in that way you will also encounter beings, or shall we say thoughts and feelings, which could lead you off your rightful course. However, as we have said, you are being deliberately led carefully towards your goals.

Bob: Right. But if I understand it rightly, the imaginative, pictorial meditations you've given could be seen rather like doorways – or opening doorways – to step into different regions of the spirit worlds. Is that right?

Joshua: Yes, that is correct, and is it a good way of putting it. The meditations form portals, entrances for you, stepping into these worlds.

Bob: And if we step into these worlds we will meet, or encounter, various beings. Correct?

Joshua: Yes, you will, but you will always have someone, a guardian, with you to help you differentiate and know who exactly you are meeting.

Bob: So, do we have the same guardian being with us throughout the journey, or different guardians at different times, or stages, on the path?

Joshua: It is actually the same guardian who goes with you, even though you do not always see him as the same one. He can take different forms.

Bob: Well, isn't that going to be confusing?

Joshua: Actually, no, because you will have the same feeling of protection and reassurance, even if the appearances vary.

Bob: Well, Joshua, I can only accept at this stage what you say, until such time as I can actually speak out of my own direct experiences.

Raja: Yes, let me also step in here, please. You see, my friend, until you actually begin this journey for yourself, whatever descriptions we give will remain somewhat theoretical. This is inevitable until you step out on the path. Then you will know for yourself what we are talking about.

Bob: Well, yes, that must be true of course. So, if I just come back to the meditations which have been given, is it a matter of immersing oneself in that picture and situation, and then seeing what unfolds from that?

Raja: Yes, it is. By doing the inner, meditative work you will be led forward, stage by stage.

Bob: This then really does require a great deal of trust, doesn't it?

Raja: Yes, again you are correct. Trust is an absolutely basic requirement.

Bob: But some people might say this is like 'blind trust', or 'blind faith' in the powers-that-be.

Raja: Yes, they could say that, but actually, through your own experiences, you are also growing in knowledge – in your own personal knowledge of these realities.

Bob: Wouldn't it be helpful to have a friend to share these experiences with, and perhaps to gain reassurance?

Raja: Well, my friend, you do have many friends in spirit with whom you can discuss these things, as indeed you are doing now!

Bob: That is true, but I was thinking of a friend on the physical plane, actually.

Raja: Perhaps you will find such a friend to talk to when you begin this work. Perhaps then – also physically – a person will appear to whom, or with whom, you can share such things.

Bob: Yes, perhaps. A further question of clarification about practice of the meditations. Is not the reason for doing these – any of them – to raise our consciousness beyond the physical level? Actually, you could say, to go out of our physical bodies?

Raja: Yes, that is correct. In a subtle way you free yourselves from the physical vehicle and thereby enter into different worlds.

Bob: But couldn't this be dangerous? Couldn't we have difficulty getting back in and grounding ourselves?

Raja: No, this is not a problem, provided you meditate properly. I mean by this, going into the meditation consciously and then, after a time, bringing it to a proper close and feeling yourself grounded again.

Bob: So, how long could – or should – we spend in the meditative state?

Raja: Each person must find out what is appropriate and possible for him or her. We would recommend not more than an hour, though it could be much less than this if circumstances demand it. You have to find out for yourselves what you are comfortable with and what, practically, is possible.

Bob: Steiner puts great emphasis on the esoteric pupil being true to the needs and values of the earthly world. By this I think he means, to our very human responsibilities in life, to ourselves and others. Do you agree with this?

Raja: Yes, we strongly agree with this. It is essential that you do this work to help you become better human beings, better members of humankind. You do not do it to run away from your responsibilities, but rather to help you to fulfil them to your best ability.

Bob: So, this again points to the importance of having a very clear – crystal clear, we could say – motive for wanting to do this work. Ultimately, to gain knowledge, self-knowledge, which helps us to know ourselves in a truly human way?

Raja: Yes, precisely so: to become self-realized human beings, acting out of knowledge and understanding of who you truly are.

Bob: By doing this work, which we can only do as individuals, does it somehow help the world; help others also?

Raja: Yes, it does, because by changing – or rather finding – yourself, you are helping to change the world. The two belong together.

Bob: So, to conclude. By taking up this Path, by stepping into spirit worlds, we can become better, more genuine, human beings.

Raja: Yes, that is right, and that is the whole purpose of the work, which you can choose, freely, to undertake.

All blessings, Raja Lampa

10.
SUMMARIZING THE PATHWAY

Summary

Let us now, in this final chapter, enumerate in a brief summary the steps which the guides have provided us with, in order to journey into spirit worlds consciously and safely. They are given below as follows, based on the teachings which were received from those particular guides. However, please also read each chapter in full in order to gain a thorough understanding.

1. *From Red Cloud*:
Due preparations of heart and mind are needed. Gaining inner quiet. Bringing the soul into proper shape and order. Control of thoughts, feelings, and actions. Self-observation and self-reflection. A 'purification process'. A gradual process, through daily working and discipline. Patience and perseverance, 'to gain the necessary balance and self-control when you no longer have the benefit of your physical body to hold everything together for you'. So, first, careful preparation before setting out on your quest.

2. *From Markos:*
Stepping over the threshold between the physical – or material – and the spirit world. How to do this consciously and be awake to your new surroundings. The need to gain the necessary strength of soul, when you no longer

have the reflecting mirror of your physical brain. The need to build a new mirror, through your own construction, through meditation. To develop a spiritual organ to perceive the spirit world around you. 'In effect, you will need to create spiritual eyes and ears, if you are to learn to see and hear in the worlds of spirit beings.'

3. *From Raja Lampa:*
The inner path of meditations. The means by which the human soul can strengthen itself to cross the threshold. Meditation is a very individual matter. Nonetheless, clear guidance and advice can be given. Be honest with yourselves regarding your motives. Also, the right mood and feelings are very important in meditative work. A specific meditation content is given which, later, is termed, the 'Door Meditation'. An imagination – visualization – is practised, and eventually, 'the door will open and you will be permitted to step through'. Requires perseverance and sincerity. The door is opened by 'the Watcher' or 'Guardian'.

4. *From Markos:*
How to proceed further from this point – of stepping through the doorway. Again, it is through the strengthening of the soul, through meditative exercises. Another meditation is needed to steer you along the right course. The spirit world is a world of beings. The way forward is by getting to know the different beings who live in these worlds. Another specific meditation is given, the 'Angel Meditation'. You are greeted, welcomed, by your angel on the far side of the threshold. Trust in, and be led, by your angel. You will actually be led towards the inner Temple.

5. *From Isobel:*
The angel has guided you to the Temple, the Sanctuary –
to that sacred place in spirit where you can meet higher
guides. We can call this new meditation, the 'Temple Meditation'; a domed building which you walk through to a
resting place. Await whoever will come to meet you there.
A holy space, in which you feel a sense of awe, wonder
and reverence. Eventually a friend, a being from the higher
hierarchies, comes to you. Be open to whatever passes
between you. Receive guidance and knowledge in humility and thankfulness.

6. *From Gopi Ananda:*
You are on a journey to come to your own true Self. This will
lead you further into higher and higher regions of the spirit
worlds. For this we give you another meditation to work at,
the 'Stars Meditation'. From the snowy mountain top, you
look upwards towards the stars. You feel yourself travelling
out from your body in order to reach the stars, which invite
you to come to them. That is, the beings who reside in the
stars. You will meet divine beings of the higher hierarchies.
Amongst these beings, 'You will also discover your own
true I'. In the starry realm you will be able to find yourself!

7. *From Pierre:*
You have come a long way in your journey into spirit
worlds. You can now enter meditatively into an experience
of being, 'at one with All That Is': a cosmic consciousness.
You now move beyond the stars. The new meditation, again
a situational meditation, was not given a specific name
in the teachings, but we can perhaps call it, the 'Cosmic
Consciousness Meditation' – a situation where all separation

drops away from you, so that you are completely merged and at one with 'All That Is'. You could also say that you feel at one with God, and therefore a God-consciousness. Try to imagine that you have come close to this Being, the One who presides over all worlds; the One who in Christian tradition is designated as, 'the Father'. This, then, is the content of your meditation. It is a feeling of immeasurable and limitless Love. 'When you reach this stage you have come to the summit, the height, of your experience of the Divine Being.' Also: 'You have achieved the self-knowledge which has been your goal from the start of your journey.'

*

So, with this, the inner pathway given by the guides has reached its culmination. It consists of the ongoing preparations of heart and mind to strengthen the soul-forces of thinking, feeling and will, together with the five meditations. In the course of it, we become aware of various spirit beings. In addition to the further questions which were asked in Chapter 8, I will now also ask the following questions concerning the practical inner work before us. That is, if we altogether choose and decide to walk this meditative path. It is always in our own freedom to decide to undertake this quest – or instead, not to do so.

Bob: Joshua, I want now to ask some more questions concerning this path to spirit worlds which the guides have described to us. Is this alright?

Joshua: Shalom, my friend. Yes, it is alright and we are ready to answer your questions to the best of our ability.

Bob: Right. Now, I know from my own experience that meditation is not as easy as someone may think!

At least, not that type of meditation which involves immersion into a certain thought-content, image or verse. There are of course many forms and types of meditations. For example, those that are especially focussed on breathing exercises – but this is not the kind I'm thinking of. In this book, the guides have given us pictorial meditations, contents in the form of images and visualizations. Also, they are 'situational', in the sense that the person is to imagine him or herself in a quite particular context. For example, standing in front of a heavy door, or going upwards to merge with the stars. So in other words, it is one thing to describe a meditation, and it is quite something else to actually do it. Do you agree?

Joshua: Yes, we do agree, my friend. As you say, doing is different from simply describing. Anyone, perhaps, can describe a pathway to somewhere, but to actually get on and walk it is something else.

Bob: So, there are various questions which flow from this. Is it necessary to do the meditations described sequentially, in the order and sequence that they have been given, or could someone just jump in where they wanted to?

Joshua: Well, the order, the sequence, is important because it is indeed a pathway which you can journey along if you decide to do so. One thing then leads to another. It wouldn't make much sense to begin at the end of the journey rather than at the beginning, would it? So yes, in answer to your question, we see the journey going through the steps which have been given to you.

Bob: But how long might this journey take to reach cosmic consciousness – to get to the goal, so to speak?

Joshua: It is impossible to answer this question. It is entirely individual how long a person's particular journey will take. However, it is the journeying itself which should be focussed upon, and the experiences which it brings. Otherwise, it is like rushing from place to place to get to the end. Rather than that, we recommend enjoying the journey, if I can put it like that; savouring the moment, rather than just rushing along to get it finished.

Bob: Yes, I can see the wisdom of that – but coming back to the doorway, the 'Door Meditation' *per se*, how long might a person wait until the door is opened and he or she gains admission?

Joshua: Once again, no time can be given for this. It is a question, a matter, of experience and of patience and perseverance – but above all else, being in the right mood. You cannot force your way into spirit worlds without risking harm to yourself and others. It has to be seen that you are ready to make this step safely.

Bob: And is this the task of the Watcher, the Guardian, to see that this readiness has been reached?

Markos: Yes, precisely so. The Guardian is there to make sure that all goes well and, therefore, that you can enter into that new dimension of experience without harm.

Bob: So, is it a question of just waiting patiently before the door? Is that the right attitude?

Markos: It is, my friend. Waiting with complete calm, knowing that when the time is right the door will open for you.

Bob: And then the angel is there to guide us further?

Markos: Yes, indeed. The angel waits to take you by the hand and walk with you along the pathway.

Bob: To the Temple?

Markos: Yes, to the Temple of light and wisdom, within which you will find the further guidance which you need to travel onwards.

Bob: So, on this pathway, this inner pathway, we are really being led and guided stage by stage?

Markos: Precisely so. You are watched over and guided carefully along.

Bob: Well, I suppose we can only go so far in talking about all this. The proof of the pudding is in the eating, so to speak. At a certain point, words need to become deeds!

Markos: They do, indeed.

Bob: But one other question. Why are the meditations given as visualizations – as images to be meditated upon, rather than words? What is the reason for this?

Markos: It is so that you already enter into a pictorial way of thinking, shall I say. You move beyond just words, which can appear rather abstract sometimes, into living images. Yes, the images and the situations need to be conjured up in your soul in as living a way as you can.

Bob: Together with the appropriate feelings?

Markos: Yes, absolutely, the feeling element is essential to the efficacy and power of the images to help you along the path.

Bob: Well, Markos, just one more question, namely: the motivation to do this work, to walk this path. Does it help the world, somehow – our earthly world – if a person earnestly goes along this way to gain knowledge and understanding of spirit realities?

Markos: It does. Yes, the whole world benefits through such individual efforts. You as an individual are a part of the world. You belong to the world. If you gain higher

75

knowledge and understanding, then – as it were by a sort of ripple effect – the world is also lifted up a step.

Bob: Isn't the goal of evolution, world evolution I mean, to become more spiritual, in the sense of a spiritualization process?

Markos: Yes, it is. It is a raising of energies, so that the darkness of matter is overcome and a new lightness of being comes about.

Bob: And this leads us closer to our own true Selves?

Markos: Yes, it does. It is an illusion to think of yourselves as purely material, physical beings. You are actually spirit beings within a physical sheath, when incarnated in earthly life. After death, the body is put aside, and you expand into the wider cosmos.

Bob: So, to go along such a meditative path as described here, is to work already on that expansion, that outward journey that everyone actually makes after death?

Markos: It is, but to do it consciously and safely whilst still incarnated on the Earth.

Bob: Last question: So, it is a path of knowledge of Self and world in its wider, cosmic sense?

Raja: Yes, it is. It is indeed a path of knowledge and also a path of self-transformation. That is to say, realizing who you really are!

All blessings

Bob: Thank you.

AFTERWORD

In the Introduction I made it clear that the purpose of writing this book with the guides was to provide an accessible and safe way to enter, consciously, into spirit worlds. It is there, in those worlds, that I believe we shall discover who we really are; not just earthly beings, but spirit beings in our own divine right. Therefore, the path to spirit worlds is also a path of true self-knowledge. Without such insight our lives can, at critical times, lose direction and sense, or at least be full of questions and enigmas. Especially so when significant blows of fate occur in our own lives or those of our loved ones. These may take the form of serious illnesses or accidents, or even a death – whether expected or quite 'out of the blue'. Through a true self-knowledge, however, we can hope to achieve a much greater sense of purpose as individuals, and play a much more effective part in helping to transform our world – particularly from a place of fear and conflict to one of genuine compassion, freedom and love.

Therefore, to follow a meditative path, such as the one described in this book, can be seen as a real deed of service for the good of the whole world, rather than as any narrow, egotistic pursuit. Certainly, if good can come from gaining a truer picture of ourselves and the other worlds in which we live, then this goal will be a strong source of motivation for us to make the efforts required to gain such spiritual insights. Ultimately, the motive and raison d'être for any striving for Truth and Knowledge should, I believe, be for the greater good of all. This may of course be considered by some as a very idealistic viewpoint, and one far removed from the real world of big business profits, materialistic success and all the latest technological wonders! However, is it not our individual and common ethical strivings that will really help us to heal the many conflicts with which our earthly world is beset? These include the conflicts between short-term goals and partisan political policies versus the long-term, ecological and global wellbeing of our world.

As I write now, in November 2021, the whole world is still plunged in the new pandemic. This at present constitutes the biggest threat to humanity *per se* and has, temporarily, overshadowed the global challenge of climate change. Whilst the pandemic is causing much suffering and loss of life, it is also bringing many changes to what we thought of as 'normal life'. Some of these changes may even prove to be very positive – not least, a new sense of collective humanity and the need for urgent international cooperation on a small planet. There may, perhaps, also awaken a new awareness and consciousness for spiritual perspectives, but rather in terms of a truly 'explorative spirituality' than depending on traditional religions and dogmas. Such a refreshing possibility remains to be fully seen, but already the pandemic has generated much genuine human warmth and compassion. Captain Tom's* efforts epitomize all this.

---

*Captain Sir Tom Moore (1920–2021) was a British Army officer and fundraiser who made international headlines in 2020 when he raised money for charity during the COVID-19 pandemic in the run-up to his 100th birthday.

So, in conclusion I would give a threefold answer to the question: 'Why would anyone wish to enter into spirit worlds in this lifetime?' My answer is: firstly, to see that the reality of the world is actually much bigger and broader than we ordinarily know. It is multi-dimensional and filled with beings on all levels of development. Secondly, that even if we accept the concept of reincarnation, where we ourselves have had multiple personalities and lifetimes – transcending all these different earthly identities is our own true spirit Self. This unique Self actually lives in spirit worlds. To really know ourselves, therefore, we need to enter those same worlds. Thirdly, through the deeper knowledge of world and Self that we have thus gained, we can aim to become more effective, more compassionate and more moral helpers of humanity. In this way, we also become conscious co-creators in the progress and evolution of both our earthly world and the wider cosmos.

Of course, we can also simply rest content with the comprehensive descriptions of spirit worlds as given by Rudolf Steiner and others, including my own guides. However, these will always remain as 'second-hand' knowledge until such time that we make the ascent into higher worlds and experience them for ourselves. As in ancient times, the guiding motto must still be: 'O Man, Know Thyself!'

In Buddhist traditions, those human beings who – through their inner work and striving – had attained enlightenment, did so in order to help liberate all sentient beings. Such was the elevated mission of the so-called Bodhisattvas and Buddhas. At the end of his autobiography, *The Path to Freedom*, the Dalai Lama shares this short prayer:

> For as long as space endures,
> And for as long as living beings remain,
> Until then may I, too, abide,
> To dispel the misery of the world.*

He says this gives him '... great inspiration and determination'.

It is also no exaggeration to say that, to the extent that each person likewise becomes a centre for inner peace and compassion, the whole world benefits through this. Clearly, if many people achieve this state, the good effects are both multiplied and magnified enormously.

It is then precisely for the healing of the world and the betterment of humankind that the pathway to higher, spirit worlds will be trodden. In this book, the guides have given us a clear route to follow. In fact, I have to say, I am very impressed and very grateful for just how clearly this path has been laid out for us. It will undoubtedly require much practice, perseverance and effort to 'walk' it. However, the ultimate benefits will surely outweigh the struggles we have to face to do this. At any event, the opportunity is there and, when we rise to the challenge, we can begin to explore exactly where this will lead us. There is certainly no outer – nor inner – compulsion to work on this. The

*The Dalai Lama, *The Path To Freedom*: *Freedom in Exile and Ancient Wisdom*, Abacus 2005, p. 314.

choice is always ours to make freely, whenever we feel sufficiently motivated to begin this existential quest. No doubt, our spirit guides are there to help us every step of the way.

All blessings, Bob

APPENDIX 1:
THE GUIDES

I have been consciously aware of my first spirit guides since 2005. In actual fact, there were just two to begin with, namely Dr John and Joshua Isaiah. However, since 2016, and in connection with writing the book *Trusting in Spirit – The Challenge*, I became aware of other guides also. Indeed, I experienced what I have described in the above book as a 'Circle of Guides' who stepped forward, so to speak, to work with me on that project. How they made their presences felt initially is recorded therein.

For this present publication, the following guides have cooperated with me, including two female guides of whom I have been aware during the past year or so. I will identify them in the order in which they make their contributions to this book.

1. *Joshua Isaiah*
   In a former life he was a Jewish Rabbi.
2. *Red Cloud*
   In a former life he was a Sioux Native American Chief.
3. *Raja Lampa*
   In a former life he was a Tibetan Lama.
4. *Philip*
   My guardian angel.
5. *Markos*
   In a former life he was a Greek monk and philosopher.

6. *Pierre*

In a former life he was a member of the Knights Templars in France.

7. *Isobel*

I understand that she was my pupil in a former lifetime in India, when apparently I was then a guru. (Clairvoyantly, to my friend Neil, Isobel took the form of a female with long blonde flowing hair and very blue eyes.)

8. *Gopi Ananda*

Likewise, she was also associated with me in that former lifetime in India. In my mind's eye I see Gopi dressed in a green sari. Her black hair is tied back, her complexion brown-skinned and a red mark is on her forehead at the position of the 'third eye'. She – and Isobel – are youngish in appearance, rather than old.

While I do understand that some readers, particularly those who have not previously met the concept of spirit guides, may find these descriptions difficult to accept, I would suggest simply to try to keep an open mind. It has also been a learning curve for me to develop the necessary trust in their realities. It is worthwhile pointing out that it is unusual, as far as I know, for so many guides to cooperate in a project. It is well known that particular guides have worked consistently with one or another medium. For instance, the many teachings channelled through Grace Cooke from her guide White Eagle, and also the teachings from Gildas given through Ruth White. I have no idea whether, in future, I will be made aware of still other guides who may wish to contribute to my writings. We will see. However that may be, I do believe that there is always a good reason why one or another guide steps forward.

It is not arbitrary, but entirely purposeful. I believe that each person has at least one spirit guide with them at any one time. That is in addition to their own guardian angel. If we become open to this idea, then we can facilitate a conscious relationship with our friends in spirit.

Interestingly, neither John – my spirit-doctor – nor Pan – the God of Nature – contributed to this enquiry. Both of them did so in my two previous books. Clearly, the most appropriate guides step forward, according to the particular subject being researched.

APPENDIX 2:
EXPERIENCES OF WORKING WITH
THE MEDITATIONS

I will here share some of my initial experiences from working with the meditative Imaginations given by my guides. However, in doing so I am mindful that each person who embarks on this path will make his or her very own individual experiences. I do not want what I write here to colour or unduly influence what each person may come to. Therefore, I will be selective and only mention some aspects of my experiences that could be supportive and interesting for others to hear about. Individuals will of course decide how often to do this inner work, since in this we are left completely free to do what suits us.

I think it is important, before beginning to meditate, to briefly remind oneself of the actual reasons for doing so. In other words, to be quite clear in one's own mind about the motivation for this. Having done so, to then enter imaginatively into the first scenario, namely to see oneself standing on one side of 'the Door'; in this and all other situation meditations, it is very important to endeavour to cultivate the appropriate attitudes and feelings. So, in front of 'the Door' to feel a certain humility, but also hope and expectation.

I find myself there dressed as a monk, wearing a grey habit. At a certain point I go forward and knock on the door, three times, and wait for it to be opened by the Guardian. When this has happened and I step over the threshold, my clothing changes from the monk's habit to a blue garment. I see my angel coming forward to welcome and to lead me along the – upward – way. Once again, I find it important to experience the appropriate feelings. Here a joyful recognition and gratitude, I would say, is very fitting.

The path leads us then towards the domed Temple. When we stand in front of it, the doors are already open and we can go inside the main hall. I see this large space as suffused with all the colours of the rainbow. It has also been my experience – a growing, developing, awareness – that many people or souls are in this place. It is a busy but unhurried place to be. I found that I met here those – deceased – people that were important in my life. There is a sense of warm greeting, welcome and recognition. You could say the Temple becomes a 'hall of souls'.

Passing then through the main space of the Temple we come to one end in which a number of doors – light not heavy doors – are located. My angel and I go into a smaller room through such a doorway. This is a place where higher guides will come, or be there, to point the way forward on this inner journey. This will then be an ascent into the starry cosmos, which I have yet to experience.

So, this I feel is what I can briefly share, so far, about this meditative journeying. It is a developing, mobile inner process. Practically, I find that my meditation takes about 35 minutes and always concludes, after briefly retracing the journey, to being outside 'the Door', once again in monk's habit. As I have said, it will be on each person to make their own experiences in working with the five Imaginations which the guides have given us. That is, if you choose to do so. Remember, as I pointed out earlier, there are two sides to working with the meditations – in the first place to actively visualize and feel oneself into the particular situation, be it at 'the Door', with 'the Angel', in 'the Temple', to 'the Stars' and into 'Cosmic Consciousness'. Then, in the second phase, to be open to how the meditations can be 'windows' into experiencing the actual spirit realities. It is a process of developing the abilities and the spiritual senses to enter into these worlds fully consciously. We can also say that we are undertaking our own research journeys into these extrasensory dimensions.

Personally, I do see this journeying as cooperating very directly with my own angel, Philip. I usually make contact with him before meditating. The following communication may be helpful to share:

Bob: Philip, I will soon enter into the Imaginations once again. Do you have any advice for me please?
Philip: Bob, my friend and brother, simply enter into the scenes and the pictures as fully as you can, really trying to put yourself into these situations. Then, see what emerges for you. It is a meditative working and process, and it will reveal its own meaning to you as you work further with it.

All blessings, Philip

In going along this way, we should, I feel, have a certain sense of joyfulness – that our own small efforts are thereby contributing to the progress and success of humanity's evolutionary pathway.

FURTHER READING

The following select literature might be helpful to some readers.

Lama, D.H.H. (2004) *The Many Ways to Nirvana*. Hodder & Stoughton.

Lama, D.H.H. (2006) *The Path to Freedom*. Abacus.

Steiner, R. (1994) *Guidance in Esoteric Training*. Rudolf Steiner Press.

Steiner, R. (1994) *How to Know Higher Worlds*. Anthroposophic Press.

Steiner, R. (1995) *Intuitive Thinking as a Spiritual Path*. Anthroposophic Press.

Steiner, R. (1994) *Theosophy – An Introduction to the Spiritual Processes in Human Life : and in the Cosmos*. Anthroposophic Press.

Steiner, R. (1999) *A Way of Self-Knowledge*. Anthroposophic Press.

Woodward, B. (2020) *Knowledge of Spirit Worlds and Life After Death*. Clairview Books.

Woodward, B. (2007) *Spirit Communications*. Athena Press.

Woodward, B. (2018) *Trusting in Spirit – The Challenge*. Author House.

MORE ABOUT THE AUTHOR

I was born in 1947 in Gloucester in the UK. At the age of eleven I had the good fortune to fail my 11-plus exam, which was then the entrance into what sort of state secondary education was available to pupils. Through this stroke of destiny, I entered Wynstones, an independent Rudolf Steiner School in Gloucestershire, where I remained for seven years until I was eighteen. Following 'A levels' in Maths and Physics, I went to university and, a year later, became a university drop-out!

At the age of 23, at Easter 1970, I was guided to become a co-worker at the Sheiling School in Thornbury, a centre of the Camphill Community based on the teachings of Rudolf Steiner (1861-1925). Apart from a year at Emerson College in Sussex, I spent some 40 years within the Camphill Movement, living with and teaching children with special educational meeds. I retired from this work in 2012.

I became a student of Steiner's anthroposophy, having first read one of his fundamental books *Knowledge of the Higher Worlds – How is it Achieved?* when I was around 18 years old, now more than 50 years ago. Later, I also became a member of the Anthroposophical Society in Great Britain. I have however always tried to keep an open mind, and I consider myself a perpetual student. When I was 46 I received an M.Ed. degree from Bristol University and this was followed by an M.Phil. when I was 50. In 2011, I was awarded a Ph.D. from the University of the West of England, when nearly 64.

As well as being a qualified curative educator, I am also a spiritual healer and an author. I took a special interest in understanding autism in children and young people.

I have a lifelong interest in philosophy and spirituality, and in exploring the existential questions of life and death, meaning and freedom. Fundamentally, I see myself as a researcher in the field of spirituality, particularly in my conscious relationships with my spirit guides over the past fifteen years and my ongoing work with them.

In 2022, I will have been married for well over 40 years to my wife Silke. We have five grown-up children and, currently, ten lively grandchildren. I enjoy walking, swimming, reading, writing, painting and tai chi! My wife and I particularly look forward to our holidays on the beautiful Isles of Scilly in Cornwall. I feel that I have received clear guidance in my own life, and am very grateful for this.